KT-441-263

Bridges

KATE PETTY and TERRY CASH

 **Photographs by Jenny Matthews** 

Contents

TRACKS

624.2 PET

A&C Black · London

S280474 (b)

Bridges around you

Does your journey to school take you over a busy road? Maybe you have to go across a railway or a river. If you do, then you have probably crossed a bridge today.

Bridges make journeys easier. If there were no bridges, you might have to swim across a river or leap across a ravine.

Or you might have to dodge between fast cars or travel out of your way. A bridge can make your journey shorter, too.

How do the bridges around you make your journey easier?

Make a collection of pictures of bridges around you. You can draw them or take photographs. See if you can find your bridges marked on a map. How old do you think the bridges are? Why were they built?

Traffic on a bridge

A bridge is built to suit the sort of traffic that is going to use it.

One of the first bridges was probably just a tree trunk lying across a stream. Other simple bridges were made of creepers tied across from one side of a river bank to another. These bridges were simple to make and could carry a person's weight, but they can't carry heavy traffic.

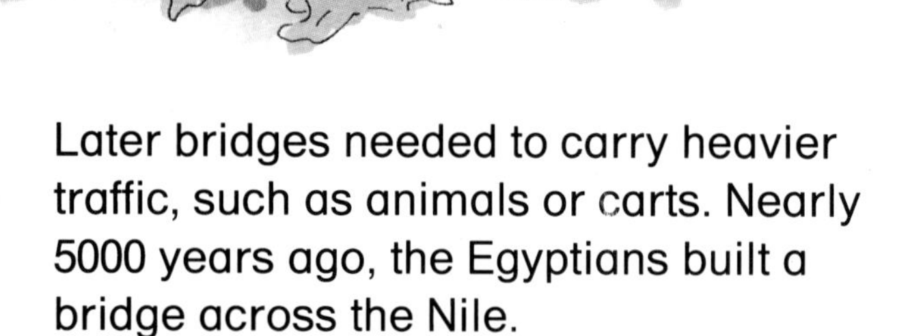

Later bridges needed to carry heavier traffic, such as animals or carts. Nearly 5000 years ago, the Egyptians built a bridge across the Nile.

Different kinds of traffic led to new sorts of bridges. The Romans built arched bridges wide enough for armies to cross. They also built huge bridges to carry water to their new towns.

In the seventeenth century, London Bridge was so large that it had shops and houses on it. You can see shops on Pulteney Bridge in Bath.

Today an old stone bridge which was strong enough for a horse and carriage might have to be widened to make room for cars to cross. A bridge which is part of a motorway needs to be wide enough for several lanes of traffic, and strong enough not to collapse under the weight of all the cars and lorries.

Can you bridge a gap?

You will need
two equal sized piles of books
two sheets of paper
a toy car

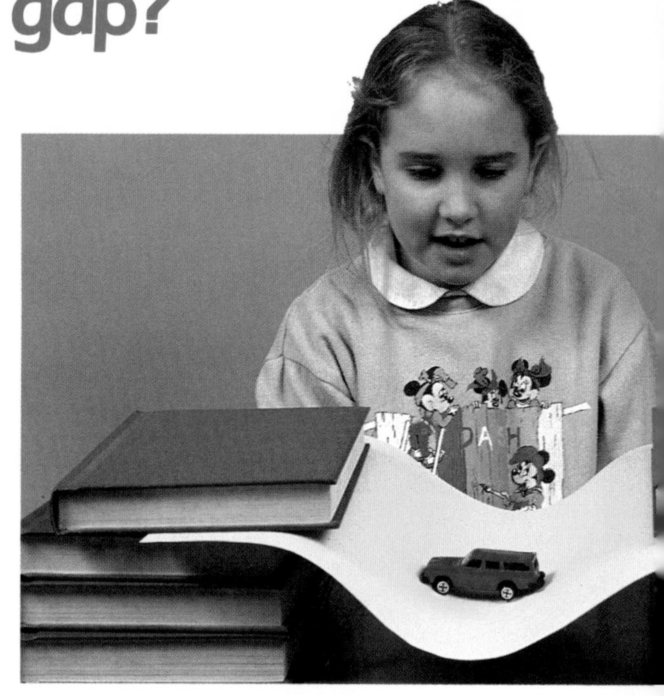

How many ways can you find to make a bridge?

This way is not very strong. How can the bridge be made stronger?

with an arch

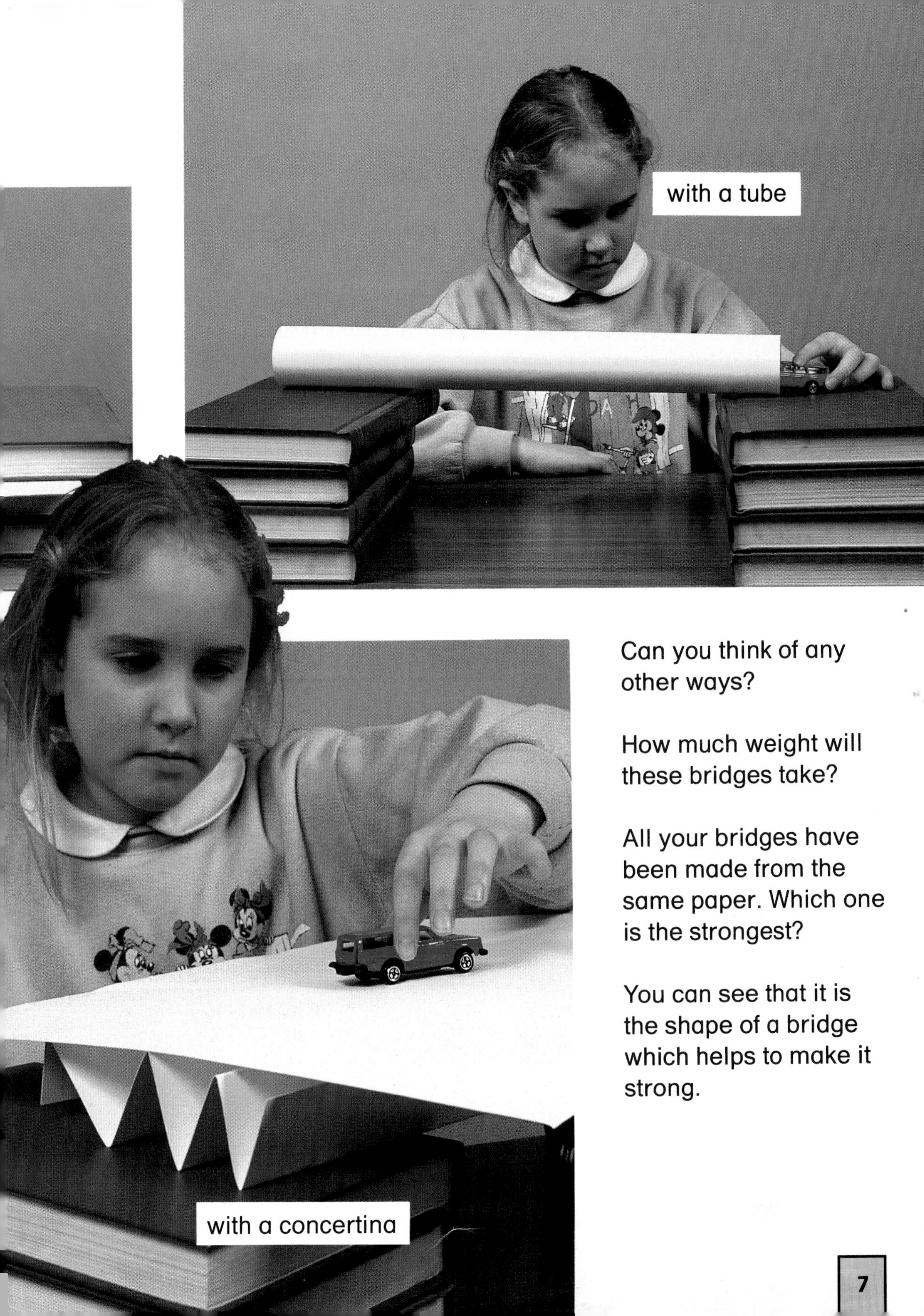

Can you think of any other ways?

How much weight will these bridges take?

All your bridges have been made from the same paper. Which one is the strongest?

You can see that it is the shape of a bridge which helps to make it strong.

Supporting a bridge

One of the simplest bridges is made by laying a log across a stream. If the banks are firm, the bridge will be strong. But what happens if the banks are a long way apart?

Supporting a long bridge

You will need
a long strip of card or a metre ruler

three chairs

Make a bridge by stretching the card from one chair seat to the other. Is this bridge strong? What happens if you put a load such as a toy car onto it? If you are outside, what happens when the wind blows?

Put another chair in the middle as a support. Is your bridge stronger or weaker?

Most bridges have to rest on supports, called piers. The piers have to be on solid ground, otherwise the bridge will sink. They take the weight of the bridge when people walk across it.

Spreading the weight

You will need
nine cardboard tubes
a tray
a friend

Look at your tubes. Do you think you can stand on them without squashing them?

Now stand your tubes on end in three rows of three. Put the tray on top. With your friend's help, you should be able to climb on the tray and stand on it, supported by the cardboard tubes!

This bridge is 2000 years old. It's made of stone slabs which are laid over piers made of heaps of stone.

Beams and girders

Solid slabs of stone are very heavy. Light materials can be just as strong, so bridge builders began to think of other ways to make strong beam bridges.

How strong is a wooden girder?

You will need
a long thin strip of wood or
a metre ruler

some pieces of
plasticine as weights

two chairs
a bucket

Lay the wooden strip across two chairs on its flat edge to make a bridge. Slide the bucket handle along to the middle of the wooden strip. What happens to your bridge? What happens if you add some weights to the bucket?

Now do the same experiment, this time with the wooden strip on its narrow edge. Now what happens when you hang the bucket on the wood? Which way is the strongest?

A bridge can be strengthened if by resting it on long narrow supports called girders. If you look under some bridges you can see rows of girders. Box girders are long hollow supports, which can be made of steel or concrete.

Soldiers on the march need to have a bridge light enough to carry. They use a girder bridge called a Bailey bridge. Only the bare bones of the girders are used, but the bridge is very strong. Do you know any other bridges built using girders?

The strength of the arch

What sort of bridge do you build if you only have small stones or bricks? Builders discovered that a strong bridge can be built in an arch shape from wedge-shaped bricks.

An arch-shaped bridge can support heavy loads because the weight of the load in the middle of the arch is spread down the sides to the piers.

Arch bridges have to be built around a support, which is taken away when the bridge is finished. The bricks press against each other to keep the structure together. An arch is useless until the middle stone is put in position. This stone is called a keystone.

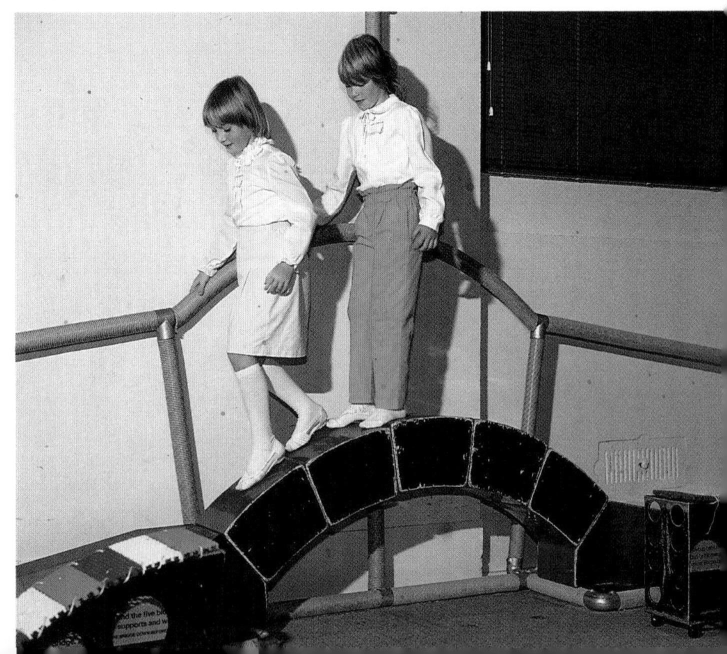

These children have built a bridge out of foam wedges. The arch is so strong that it supports their weight without any glue or cement.

Build a model arch bridge

You will need

Use the plasticine to make wedge shaped bricks. The board is the bridge support. Lay your bricks side by side to make an arch shape.

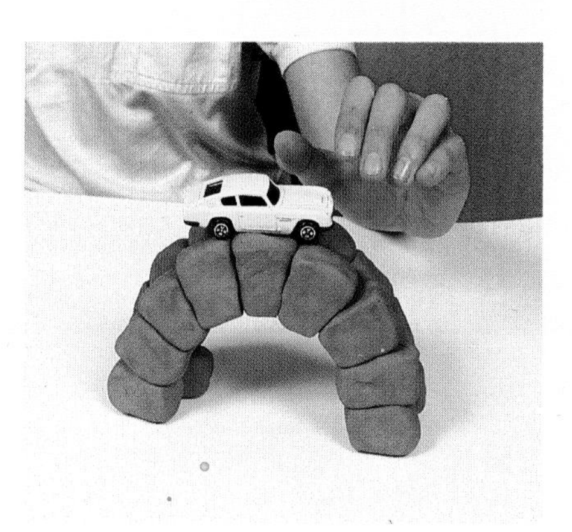

When you have put in the keystone, you can take the board away. The bridge will stand by itself. How much weight will your bridge take?

The Romans made huge arch bridges. Some are still standing after two thousand years. This bridge is an aqueduct for carrying water.

Cantilever bridges

A very long bridge can be built using lots of arches. But sometimes the supports can get in the way of what goes *under* the bridge.

To solve this problem, engineers can use a cantilever bridge. The cantilever has a strong support with one or two arms.

This bridge is a cantilever. It has nothing to hold it up in the middle. How do you think it is supported?

One of the most famous cantilever bridges is the Forth Bridge in Scotland, opened a hundred years ago. It looks like a row of giants holding hands across the water. It is a railway bridge made from thousands of tonnes of steel tubes rivetted together.

The bridge is painted with special paint to stop it rusting. As soon as the painters finish painting the bridge, they have to begin all over again.

Hanging bridges

How do you bridge a chasm? The earliest suspension bridges were rope bridges slung from one side of a ravine to another. On a bridge like this, the walkway hangs down from its supports. As long as it is firmly anchored at either end of the bridge, it doesn't matter if it sways and wobbles a bit in the wind.

The roadway of a modern suspension bridge hangs from steel ropes. The ropes are suspended from steel cables which run between tall towers. The cables are spun out of thousands of strands of steel wire and are incredibly strong.

Make your own suspension bridge

You will need

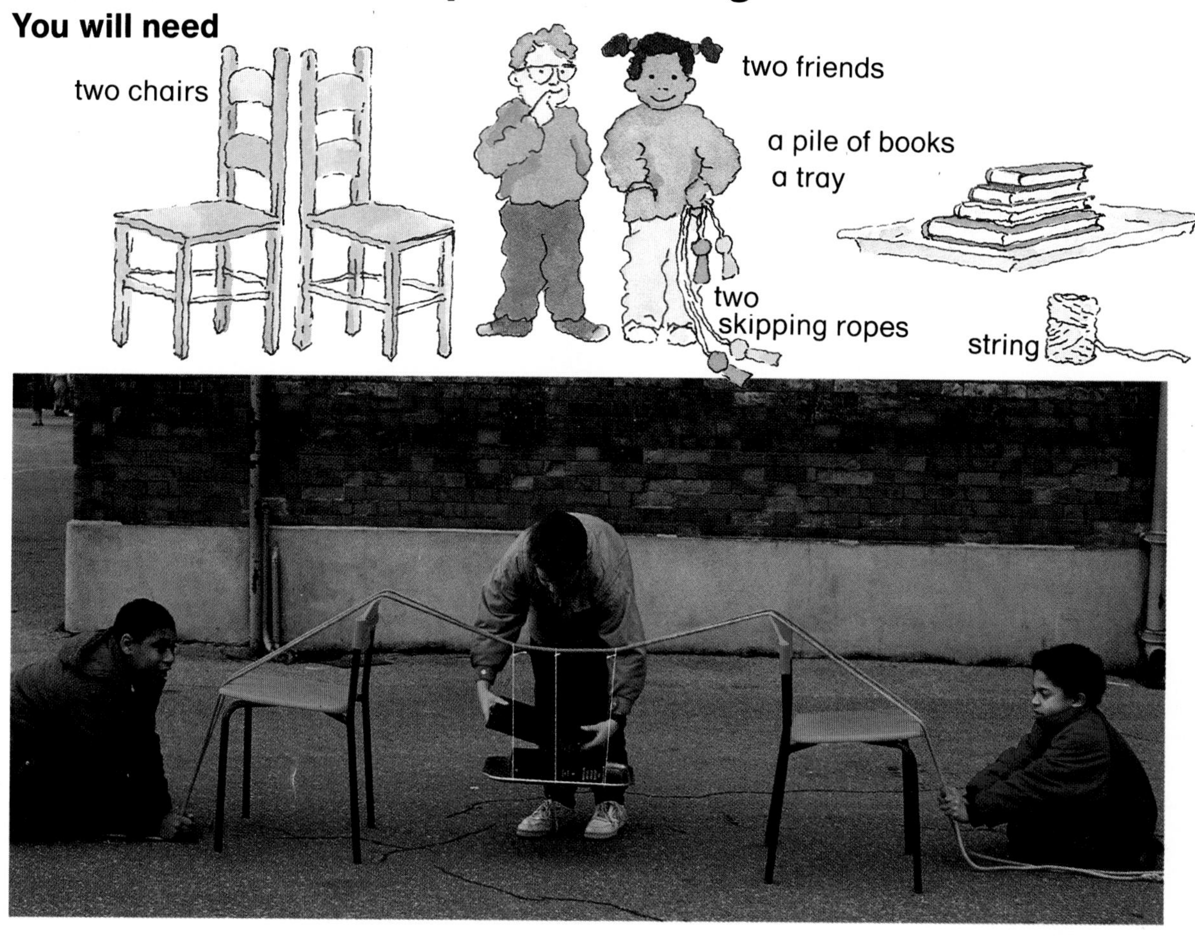

Put your chairs a short distance apart, and join them by running the skipping ropes between them. Ask a friend to hold each end of the skipping ropes on the ground. Use the string to hang the tray from the skipping ropes. Then start to load the books on to the tray. How much weight will your bridge hold? What happens if the ropes aren't held down firmly enough?

Your friends have to hold tight to keep the skipping ropes down. On a suspension bridge, the cables are attached to steel rods and buried in concrete blocks deep inside the rock at each end of the bridge.

The right materials

A bridge needs to be built from the right materials – materials which won't sag or crack or crumble under pressure.

Some of the first bridges were made from stones, logs or even creepers. Old stone bridges were solidly built and many have lasted for centuries.

The first iron bridge was built over 200 years ago. In 1826 the first suspension bridge was built, hung from chains made of wrought iron. The coming of the railways in the nineteenth century meant that many more bridges were needed, built of materials strong enough to support the trains. The first steel railway bridge was built in 1874, only a year before the building of the first concrete bridge.

Nearly all modern bridges in this country are made from steel and concrete, which can both be shaped before they set hard. The concrete is strengthened inside with steel rods. These materials are used because they are strong, hardwearing and cost-effective. Other materials have been used and bridges in the future could be made of carbon fibres or plastic.

Before a bridge is opened to the public, it is tested to see how much weight it can take. A heavy weight is hung from the bridge and then released suddenly. Instruments record how much the bridge wobbles after the weight has dropped.

Bridges also have to be able to stand winds, storms and even earthquakes. This model of a bridge is being tested in a wind tunnel to see how the finished building will stand up to being blown around.

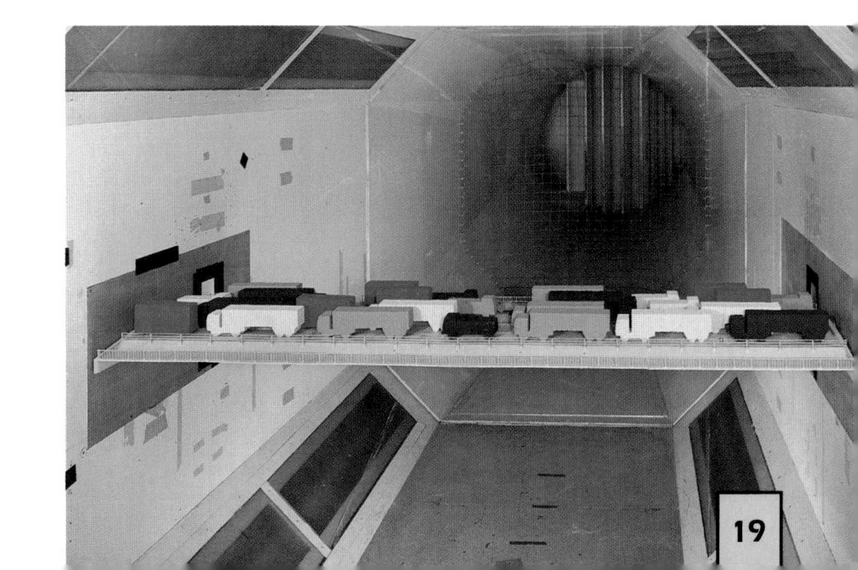

Bridges that move

Sometimes it is useful to have a bridge that can be moved out of the way. The drawbridge over a castle moat could be raised to stop invaders in their tracks.

When Tower Bridge, in London, was built over a hundred years ago, tall ships sailed up the Thames from the sea. When a ship approaches, barriers can close the road way to traffic, and the two sides of the roadway can be raised to let the ship through.

Moving bridges are often built over busy city rivers where there is a lot of traffic on the water as well as on the roadway. A swing bridge works rather like a gate. It swings to one side when river traffic needs to pass.

Make a swing bridge

You will need

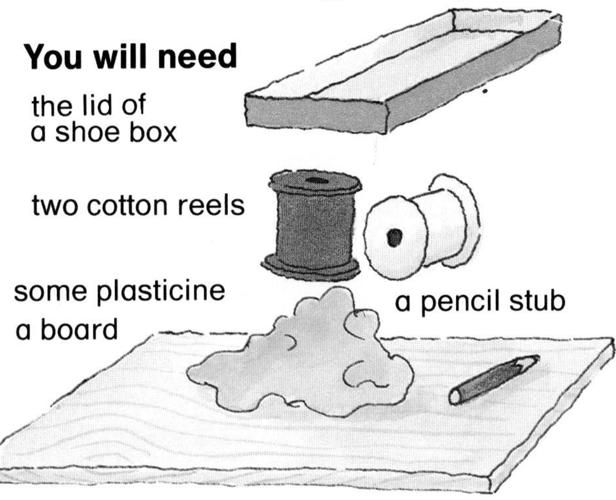

Use the plasticine to stick one cotton reel to the board. Put the pencil stub in the middle of the cotton reel. Stick the other cotton reel to the end of the box lid and place it over the pencil stub. You can now swing your bridge from side to side.

How a bridge is built

These pictures show stages in the construction of the Humber Bridge in the north of England, which has the longest span of any suspension bridge in the world.

These foundations give you some idea of the enormous scale of the bridge. Deep and solid foundations are very important.

Underwater foundations were dug using watertight containers inside which work could be carried out on the riverbed. Eventually the containers were filled with concrete to form the bases of the towers.

Concrete towers, 163 metres high, were built onto the foundations. This one has reached the level where the road is going to be.

Metal 'saddles' were fitted to the top of each tower, for the cables to run over. The cables were spun from steel across the tops of the towers and anchored in rock and concrete at either end. Steel ropes were suspended from the cables.

The deck was made from hollow box girders. Each one was towed into the river and attached to the hangers. The road now runs over the deck.

The bridge took nine years to build.

Facts

The **oldest** bridge in the world was built **c.850 BC**. It spans the River Meles in Izmir, Turkey.

The **longest** bridge in the world is the Pontchartrain Causeway in Louisiana, USA. It is **38.4 km** long.

At **350 m** wide, the Crawford St Bridge in Rhode Island, USA is the **widest** bridge.

The Royal George Bridge in Colorado, USA is the **highest** bridge. It is **321 m** above the Arkansas River.

The Humber Bridge in Yorkshire is the **longest suspension bridge** at **1,401 m**. A bridge of **1,780 m** is being built in Japan, linking the islands of Honshu and Shikoku. It is due to open in 1998.

The **longest concrete arch bridge** is in France. The Brotonne Bridge over the River Seine is **320 m** long.

The Quebec Railway Bridge over the St Lawrence River in Canada is the **longest cantilever bridge** at **549 m** long.

Two bridge disasters

In 1879, a year after it was built, the Tay Bridge in Scotland collapsed in high winds. A train crossing the bridge plunged into the river below, killing 75 people. Engineers working on the Forth Bridge in Scotland were able to learn from the Tay Bridge disaster and made sure that the new bridge could withstand strong winds.

In 1940 another bridge collapsed because of high winds only four months after it was built. It was the Tacoma Narrows Bridge in Washington, USA. Luckily no one was hurt.

London Bridge

Many bridges have stood on the site of the present London Bridge. There were probably several wooden bridges before the famous stone bridge, with its shops and houses and a drawbridge was built. The stone bridge took 30 years to build, and until 1739 it was London's only bridge across the Thames. Water rushed through its narrow arches with such force that it became a highly dangerous place for boatmen to negotiate. It was replaced in 1831 with a bridge built by Charles Rennie. His bridge now stands in Arizona, USA, where it was rebuilt by an American. The present rather plain bridge was built in 1967.

Index